When You Say One Thing but Mean Your Mother

When You Say One Thing but Mean Your Mother

poems

Melissa Broder

AMPERSAND BOOKS

an imprint of ampersand press

ISBN 13: 978-0-9841025-4-9
ISBN 10: 0-9841025-4-9

First Edition

Published by Ampersand Books
St. Petersburg, FL.
www.ampersand-books.com

Set in Mercury.

Cover design and illustrations by Benjamin Gibson.

for Nicholas

CONTENTS

Jewish Voodoo

Mother buys you an ovum mezuzah
from the fertility museum of Great Neck,
wrapped up in cheesecloth and chicken schmaltz, labeled:
Extract embryos from the icebox.

Turn her womb aquarium.
Fashion grandchildren out of ghost placenta.
Avoid white bread. Pass over Passover
for Mother's Day encore.

No kids! you shout, and maniac steamroll it
out of there, only to find your very self
back on Saturday, rummaging through her purse
for the history of your body.

What were you like as a child?
you mean to ask her, but it comes out:
Were you always this neurotic?
You want to call her *darling,* but your lips

grow foreskin thick as pomegranate casing
and down come the plagues: thunder, pestilence, lice.
For Chanukah, you'll learn to play nice;
sculpt her a golem each night.

Last Call

A car culture rumbled down
in the valley and she gave him her couch.

Drunk days clung together in the desert
suburbs; they fell down stairs holding hands.

Clutching his guitar, he sped
through the dark in neon board shorts

to the public pool, where he climbed
the chainlink fence. Why wasn't he lifted

like she got lifted? A puppet
re-strung. Did no one deliver

the message? *God looks out through your eyes.*
Men sold Tecate, limes and sticky smack,

the telephone rumored of midnight sluts
and what they did in vacant parking lots,

hard with Aqua Net and Charlie, rubbing
up against somebody. She heard

his song at Westside Grocery
and saw a sudden woman, reflected

on the freezer door. Always a girl
in the song and a few at the bar.

Core vs. Flex

Madame Famine is hairless apart
from her lanugo, and when she sucks you into
her glory hole, a bald telephone, it's

wrong. You're supposed to be the one who's lived
a thing or two, you're supposed to be teaching her
to grow. There's no room to live inside

her little Grey Gardens, so try and
let go. Stop lining up lacy aprons
with training bras and just have a damn happy

accident. You are frightened of going
over. You are not as fragile as you think.
Madame Famine should be left to rot in her

dream car with a frozen Jenny Craig
glazed salmon. Of course, she would rather
ride the bumper cars with your husband.

We Will Find Ourselves Hating a Blonde Stranger

Forget the field hockey fillies
and cotillion colts we grew up with in Greenwich,

Gladwyne and Chappaqua. In Lithuania
they'd be obsolete and we'd split hairs on our terms

over who is holy and who's stopped bleeding.·
Now we lose it different over cream cheese

thighs, lip hairs and moles the color of kishka,
going up against fawns. We have no business

playing lacrosse. The Boca *altar kakers*
with road map lipstick, Barbara Streisand bobs

and chocolate egg cream straws will tell us
that's the straightest way to the sanitarium.

When the tow-headed strangers attended
our Bat Mitzvahs in schleppy paisley sundresses

we trembled big in black, with some appetite.
What was expected of us but to stay sane?

Plenty of things. Abstain from honey-baked ham,
Nantucket, seersucker, Volkswagen,

Bloody Marys, Laura Ashley, turning
the other cheek and the non-Ivy League.

Forgive the expectors. But remember the moles
and hairs came from them. The moles and hairs make us

lose it faster than nowheresville and to lose it
is the same, with or without a suntan.

Prayer of the Teenage Waifs

We want security and we want out!
The groceries have cobwebs. French toast sticks
and sickie chicken sausages turn lettuce
for breakfast. Put dinner in a locket,
then sniff to get to clavicle heaven
where Mommy gets pinched and shock treatments
are ice capades, Sweet'N Low sensations

of Fatherland. Oh Fatherland! She's been
a bad babysitter. Deliver us
from Burger King with *People* magazine.
Let the basement be our basement, the bones
and ringtones our only breath in mirrors;
let mammaries unbloom, let fumes be food
and we'll massacre into cylinders.

Margaret Sanger Never Said

anything about vomiting.
How at the end my guts stand up

because they played the starring role.
But first I compliment the doctor

on her earrings. *From Maine? Really?*
Splayed like a lobster on its back,

I charm. Then I go to Mars.
Next I'm at a parlor party

of ginger ale and saltines
with eight other lovely ladies.

And that's where my guts go curtsy.

Why She Lets Him Go to Reno and Sleep with Whores

She knows what it is to want

to see new color nipples once
in a while, unporn, off the glass

of the new Sony hi-def they bought
for their non-schtupping comfort; one schtup
every other Sunday night,

over pad thai and sticky rice,
as a hothouse starlet makes herself

on camera with a full set
of acrylic nails. She would
sleep with his whores if she could

detach a pair of nipples
from the story they're bound with

like strawberries on a summer
dress, an American man
and his Americanness;

if she got off on swollen hips
instead of pixeled tits, preferred

thighs to crappy plot lines, she would
bump up to live girls and play Daddy
as well. She believes he will

treat them like a gentleman,
then come back to Manhattan

where she'll show a little skin.

The Cost of Acquiring a Franchise Man

Big Ro' is Aryan, birthmarked,
bowlcut from Hair Barn, manning
Arnie's Burgers. *Forget Merle Haggard*

and Working Man Blues, I gush,
dish to me about fish filets
at laser speed, the will

of the common man, the stomachs
of the masses. He says: *Babe*
fast food life is bad-ass, cookin'

bum meth in company pots
and makin' up plots to get kids
buyin' it. I chime in:

Brand marketing! He brings pickles
from the Fixins' Bar and I ride
his knee. He burns my initials

in his arm with his Camel stub
and they sizzle like tiny burgs,
tinier than the three-for-one

minis. Hamburger Pez.
When he finger-bangs me
badly, they dance around

his bicep. *Ohhh*, he moans.
Yes, I groan. *Baby*, he moans.
Baby, I groan, *it tolls for thee.*

When he finishes, I cry.
Is it my goatee? he asks.
It isn't you, I soothe,

it's cable news.
He goes and shaves
and soon all the ladies

have their legs around his waist,
bumping the bum meth
off his bum, eating my pickles

and performing unspeakables
with ketchup and mayonnaise.
Arnie's promotes him

to slaughterhouse man, and I claim
my advertising finesse
made this monster meaty.

Truth is, they promote him
because he's big. When he makes
manager, he gets bigger.

The Amma Affair

A crowd of white Manhattanites
affix themselves to Amma's *prasad*
as if the Amma shop is Amma: magic

crystals, Amma soap, Amma saris,
Amma stickers. The crowd is *oming*
and *shanti*ing, even though nothing

is happening. Then Amma arrives
and they get grave as Greta Garbo
and you wonder if Amma, Divine

Mama, is really feral Durga
who cuts through people with her swords
to get to the skull of the matter.

You climb to the balcony dead
center, looking down at Amma,
when the sitar tells you you're lonely.

Amma starts hugging the lovelies
and uglies, and it churns your blood
like a tab of blotter dropping,

a sky writing plane spelling:
Surrender Dorothy, surrender Dorothy.
Amma is a rose and you might

just leave the planet, or hit your knees
and learn to surf. At this dose
you might forget your cell phone.

Meet Your New Counselor

Old man elbows says, *We got a fruit loop*
in from Arcata, California
and you hustle to the cafeteria

to stake out awakening, jump your jean shorts,
pay worship to this hippie phenomenon
but she is more crow's feet than feathers, Aqua Net

than braids, more Coppertone than neon Day-Glo
face paint. She says she eats meat in tacos,
spaghetti and pancakes, and gives her gun

a blow. In the trunk of her truck she keeps
no kale, only pixie sticks and Carnation
instant breakfasts. It's anybody's guess

whether she holds the door to the planet
but does she ever have pills. A republic
of laquer candies rests in a bone box

for showstopping dreamtime, there's no shortage
in that department. You cut archery
and pop an uppie with grape bug juice, let it roll,

go primate and write subversive letters home.
Dear Mommy, The macramé looks super
but really who are you? It's your own private

Jonestown in cabin two. Nothing's sprouting
sores and the disease is real cute. It smells
of sloppy joe and strawberry Charleston Chew.

Soup

When the Second Avenue Deli becomes
a bank he gets the flu. I make him Jewish

penicillin, me—a vegetarian—
ripping chicken off the bone; a blizzard

of egg noodles, parsnips and martyrdom.
He stops crying about his muscles,

I start looking at real estate listings.
A year later his immune system goes bankrupt.

The liver doc says: *liver*. The blood doc: *blood*.
The shrink calls it: *psychophysiologic*.

But I am going to heal him with pea soup,
conjure up some babushka spirits

from shtetl realms and make it all better.
The docs cook him good with a teaspoon

of Galantamine, a half cup of globulins,
simmer and blend. He can't get out of bed.

I make lobster bisque. I make potato leek,
chicken chili, beef and bean, alphabet.

Everyone, it seems, has ingredients
to recommend. A shaman in Ithaca

Uncle David went to see. Homeopathy.
A D.O. with a radio show. Saltines.

Unhitchery

Soon Ann Simons runs me backward down the street,
pee running up my leg. Soon we unsqueak

the bedsprings while your Ma lies next door, absorbed
in her Corinthians. Soon. Soon I drop out

of my own poem; the skull on the wall
reverts into an antelope, its heart

itching for the woods. Soon the incense sticks
unburn, the air conditioner returns

to Carrier's brainstorm soon. Soon the street
crosses a car, *The White Album* comes before

Rubber Soul, the L train stuffs itself
in Canarsie. Soon you get hungry

for what you never used to have. The star
of *Mamma Mia!* stops the music

and says: *When I was a child I didn't get
enough attention. Okay, I got too much*

attention. Soon the accident happens
after the news. Andy Warhol stays

dead. The mouth pours the mead. Soon the cars
are beaten by the horses rusting.

Dear Aging Anarchist

How do we put this gently? A rabble-rouser
and a baby punk, from the next generation

of revolutionaries, come down
in the Hair Care aisle at Duane Reade.

They bicker between nods, in prefab Che
t-shirts, about the proper way to make

dreadlocks: with gels or creams, creamy gels,
dreamy hells. Welcome home. We're sorry

it's not pretty. Remember the drug dream you had
in '79, where New York City

got silent sometimes? It died this evening.
Now there is a word for everything.

Inked

Prisoners do it. Men in vans by light of dash,
in squats with a dirty needle—motor, no cries,

soft cries, crying—transformation complete.
You will never work at Wal-Mart, on Wall Street,

a switch flipped. A souvenir. Stares everywhere
the next day and every day after.

At the laundromat, buying cigarettes.
He used to have parents. A raven's wing

is graying on your cheek. Learn to love it
and relearn to love it. Wake up naked,

an infant. In public pools and mirrors
remember again: when you were young

you believed you'd be the same forever.

The Tall Lady Never Not Doing Laundry

Always inhaling Sunlight,
Dynamo, Ultra or Bold.
Reducing fading, fighting
for the bright! Double concentration:
what could be more refreshing?

Never again press close in winter
coats to taste him of Marlboro
and Rumple Minze, breathing through his nose.

Always going vacationing
on an Arm & Hammer; the whitest
whites looking light, while advances
in science inspire undies
to live happier lives.

Never again thrown down and splayed
good on the city soccer field,
rubbing against his mushrooming.

Always hearing the humming
of the robust spinning tubs.
Non-corrosive stainless steel
is powerful, but gentle,
for an evening of tumbling.

Never again hump his hands
and clutch findings, murmuring
'no stopping' and meaning it.

Always sudsing in hot water
with double stain-lifter, folding
sheets and hanging jeans. Cotton
won't shrink from the quickening friction.
Fluff it, pat it, crease and repeat.

Just Like Teach for America

Your visa finally arrives
for junkie-movie studies, only

they don't send you to *Trainspotting*,
Rush or *The Basketball Diaries*

but to Washington Street, Baltimore,
and it's grim, baby, grim. At the front door

of the petri dish stands junkie Lurch,
six-foot-ten, in dustbin tuxedo

and punched-out top hat, sticks for studs.
He's sniffing glue and stuttering: *I must*

beat you up, lest you inform me
why you love junkies so much.

You say: *That's easy! Because they float above*
the sidewalk, and he says: *Wrong*, then kicks

your camera. *Oh wait*, you cry,
I got it! Because everyone's parents

are wicked. He grimaces: *Nope*,
and spits a phlegm blossom on your arm.

Now you're stumped. You worship them, that's all.
But it's junkie koan and Lurch

is Zen master here. *Listen up, Lurch,*
I've got my own doughnut-shaped holes

inside. I too hated lacrosse
as a child. There's not enough nicotine,

and the IKEA cafeteria
makes me want to find a vein. Lurch

pulls out his thingie and you plead:
Lurch, Lurch, are cotton sores sacred

like silence? He contemplates and starts
to stroke it. You want musky armpit scents

at dusk, always did. You want them
to tie you off at elbow, crank it up,

bang it in. You want family
with a capital H, den mama

home cooking up the witch, stroking
your hair as you daven all over

a burnt mattress. But Lurch is peaking
and using you for television.

Your Mother Is Dying and I Want Details

Now she's getting closer.
When you call, I salivate

for updates, last regrets,
the stench, a cellular

twinkling: not enough
battery power left

to run radio, spiders
of unbeing, as if

through some aperture
you will catapult me

underneath her skin
to walk the girders

of her skeleton
and I'll be the next

to know what.

HAIR Makes You Feel All Jesus-y

Instinct is to pull away and say we all know
what happened to the hippies, they're at IKEA,

Starbucks or dead, but is that true? You pocket
your Playbill, a stray daisy and the penises

of five leading men: Woof, Berger, Claude,
Hud and Tribesman #1. At dawn

in a big brown bed, the cosmic waterbearer
Aquarius beseeches your husband

with a gargantuan sudsy banana, thrumming
thrumming thrumming your leg, and you're thrust

out of this singular dimension, maybe
forever, a subway rocketing through space

between Brooklyn and the Island, emancipating
traffic crawl, wide open enough for all

the grinning freaks and the scowlers too
if they'd stop pushing: Amen! Shalom!

Oy vey! Krishna! Time to meet Mother
at West 4th Street (she calls it "The Village")

and buy her a nonfat vanilla astral dream cream
in a genius genius Grande cup,

$4.05 a pop, to show her you've forgiven her
for dropping in, tuning out and turning off.

Adult Onset Acne

It's luxury problem
numero uno, fear
and guilt lasagna, shame
about shame. Damn it! I'm vain.
I'm wearing sunglasses

in the supermarket,
mourning follicular fallout,
getting pus on all the towels.
It's comedones, fried shrimp,
frigidity. It's Harvard

dermatologists toying
with hypodermics and lancets,
calling it *extraction*.
What is it really? Popping zits.
It's a never-believer

in doctors, flopping over
in their rubber mitts like a drunk
over a toilet, moaning:
Take it all. It's a moist washcloth
romancing tender chin skin

under the scalding tap.
It's counting blackheads to keep track
and making plea bargains: *Three
on the right side, five on the left.
Ok, seven on the left*

but that's it! It's hormones,
sebum, dairy, stress, cosmetics,
masturbation. It's my mother
whining: *Don't pick or you'll get scars
that'll last until your wedding.*

It's revisiting starvation
to compensate, peeling face
to save face. It's a kinship
with adolescent boys,
young pustules-a-go-go, moping

home from private school in pore brine.
Should we swap medicines
and suck necks? It's the same virus.
Let's storm your parents' penthouses
and nest. Let's pop 'em in their bed.

Under the DM Tonight

The other side of good health
is gravy, I'm certain,
as Mom slips me the rectal

and sips of Robitussin
cherry suspension,
already surfing the wake

of a *Price is Right*-
Lite-Brite-Sudafed
jag. It's the end

of the old I AM,
a brand new –ism. Pray
it doesn't fade in minutes.

There are many medicines
for the taking
but just a few will take.

Grown-ups all get head transplants;
only pity ice creams
for me and my starlike ache.

What the Hell Happened to You?

The polar ice caps are melting
and in thirty years
Harry will still be worrying

about his new nose.
The nose is finicky
on Muni, on BART,

at the bar (he drinks
Stella through a straw)
and with shish kebab.

If we meet my family
they'll disturb its boundaries.
I think I want Harry

to be normal, but it's the nose
I go shopping for:
Double Rainbow rum raisin,

a Ramones shirt from Villains,
bok choy at The Slanted Door.
The nose understands

vistas make me nervous
when I say: *Life is hard*
riding shotgun at Big Sur.

Always was, says the nose
and speeds up the car.
It goes gaga for Nepenthe

and the hot tubs at Esalen,
then sits zazen at the zendo
to forget what it's been.

The Wait for Cake

You have mixed feelings
about suicide prevention.
If a person wants to go

why not let her go?
Then again there might be
another way to live

she hasn't considered
yet and a stranger to impart
these choices in a voice

paved with old potted coffee.
It's like that Bluff Point wedding
you wanted to leave

before they served the cake.
Your ride was ready to split
but the fat girl in your party

had never tried canoli cake.
Well damn her for wanting
and damn you for saying:

The fat girl. She wasn't fat
on the ride up when you talked
Hart Crane and Kurt Cobain

and which one was sexier:
drowning or shooting?
Hanging is righteous

if you can swing it, she said.
You liked her then.
But an agreement had been made:

10 pm, cake or no cake.
You knew nothing
of the catering boy

with a steel stud through his tongue,
fingering a packet of pills.
He watched you scowl

at the garter toss, mouth wet
with little lemon sorbets
and broiled fish.

When a person wants to go
why not let her go?
Stay for cake and get kissed.

Tradition

When we get hitched there will be no cake feed,

no first dance to *Feeling I'm Falling*,
no bandmaster announcing our entrance

as Mr. and Mrs. X. *The thing
about tradition*, said a very married friend,
you only get one chance to do it big.

When we divorce we will be a part
of an American tradition,
a grand incision. How will it feel
to live in the percentages? Don't be afraid

of blue days, ghostly fridges. Pain is
the touchstone of progress, and this tradition
we can really sink our teeth in, do it twice
or three times even, maybe with each other

like Taylor and Burton. On the good years
we'll invite our lawyers over for Scrabble
and Kung Pao chicken. On the off years we'll
call each other to check in. *How is*

the loneliness? I watch Letterman.
I miss your glasses. I miss kissing
off all of your lipstick. We'll compare

dates and complain about therapists.
She called me manic. So many Republicans.

I miss your applesauce. I miss your night sweats.

Is It Organic?

She beams and bites a mung bean
in half. *Well,* she says, *it's like
we collect all this stuff*

to fill us up, right?
*But in the end when we get
to see the Wiz, we'll realize*

he was always hella in us.
Yeah, I say, *I knew that.*
I reach in my trick sack

for a nicotine patch
and a bottle of Klonopin.
How else to remember

this little lemon zinger
outside the health food restaurant?
It takes a car crash.

In the meantime remember this:
Don't trust weathermen.
Don't share lipstick.

Isn't It Necromantic?

Did you vomit in my shower? asks the gentleman
who isn't her husband. His razor blades,
lavender soap and sea sponges are crusted

in warped pudding, the way the ground appears flying
over Tulum. It's strange dirt, the same that follows her
into the bathtub nightly, defiling porcelain, forcing

her maid to threaten she'll quit. On the surface
her skin is clean, creamed, fragrant with violet, cloaked
in constellations of bright blue bruises

from dancing, walking, anything that shakes
the blood so thinned by gin. At a ladies bathhouse
she first bled earth, and since then, in bodies

of water it comes in clods. How to explain this
strange dirt to a gentleman, when it baffles her?

Sweet Spot

She started recovering
when she couldn't stop

crying at the cowboy
movie. Faith is a muscle

like the rotator cuff.
After the matinee

she saved soiled tissues—
roses in her coat—

remember that sadness
won't make you explode.

Past the concession stand
taxis split open.

Falling Off the Richter Scale

When he finds his inner skaterboy
on Highway 1, he thinks he's the first
balding tourist to rediscover pubescence
at the foot of the Marin Headlands. Now

San Francisco distends to make room for him
and his brand new Tensor Lo 5.0
skateboard parts, surfboard on back-order, Oakley
blinkers, pocket *Dharma Bums*, as he drinks

Anchor at Vesuvio, brushes asses
with the young ladies of Columbus, buys bad weed
from the pavement teens on Upper Haight and good stuff
from the medical place at Fillmore Street.

He becomes himself (no really this is it
this time) at a Tantric yoni seminar
and DJ's a solstice rave until dawn.
Saint Francis has always been his man.

Then the skateboard is crushed by a produce truck
on Page and it reminds him of his last job
in New York real estate. Mark Twain was right:
he needs a warmer jacket. His new lady

leaves him for the wrong side of Market Street, home
to loonies, Moonies, old-fashioned addicts
and a tent city (she's always wanted
to live in a tent city, likes the smell
of dandruff). Soon she'll be mayor. The young

yuppies have serious Sauvignons and blondes
to carouse around with here, and they swill
in lit windows on Nob Hill to make the stars

above Grace Cathedral disappear. He doesn't
go back to City Lights but hibernates
in his rented room, far from the Jim Joneses
and graphic designers of the modern fog,

swathed in telenovelas and Double Rainbow
from the container. The Spanish were insane
to build a fort at the Golden Gate and The Dead
are dead. There's a landfill being made.

Booking Your Resurrection

The antidote began the species. Then came
Jim Jones, Jim Bakker and a travel agent
in heaven who engrossed you with Mallomars
for seventeen years.

When you resurfaced at your corner deli
on 21st and planet Earth, the night Sikh
no longer carried Little Debbie's Snack Cakes.
He forgot your face.

You are already forgiven. You know that,
don't you? Once you ate paper in Science class
to make people laugh. Love alone, totally
sane, illumined you.

Where Is Your Vampire?

In gym I scrape my knee but tear
nothing, a fresh blood bruise pooling
under wool stockings
like hickeys. A thought precedes

the wretched feeling: *Send me
somebody undead to bless
this walrus body.* On the bus
I stab a five-pointed star

into my arm with Bic ink
and a sewing needle. Doesn't
take. At eleven, it's a curse
to be only bloody

human. At twelve, it gets worse.
I'll have to pierce my own
bellybutton. In the movies,
reanimated dreamboats

fall in love with loners
but the loners are always
waifs. I eat my third dinner
on the butterfly rug:

leftover custard, yellow cake
and peanut butter spooned
straight from the container.
If I try to throw up

I must stab the heart of my throat
with a toothbrush, dig big
for cemetery belly,
but no dessert will come.

Round the Bend

Jon sees evil spirits in crazy people.
They smell like cloves or bodies decomposing.

We are candlelit. Indian dinner on Sixth.
Fork. Knife. Civilized. Clear as windows tonight.

It's safe on this side to talk about *crazy*
like a war going on in some other country.

At home, each of us brushes against it.
Jon takes blue pills, I've got grey and pink.

Still there's strata of cuckoo, a hierarchy
for lost screws. We feel apart and above

like prisoners with better numbers, whispering:
Some folks are just sicker than others. What is it

to rip past fixing: fluorescent lighting, a fount
of visitings? Linoleum, scalp smell, plastic

cups of juice. Rubber faces, dead dialtone,
the other side at the city zoo?

Man, Age 35, Wears *Sellout* T-Shirt On Varick Street

Whatever makes an entity
definable is called *identity*.

O man, age 35, attempt
one last punch at design-y-ness,

a hot twilight in Danish screenprint,
poly-cotton blend, maybe get lucky

with *Sellout*, age 25. Is he sad
about the selling? A salesman

doesn't alter his argument
if the customer is nibbling.

This is him forewarning the street,
like announcing to a packed bar:

Look at my herpe! Is it possible
to steal identity? Let's sprinkle

some holy water and resurrect
a former activist/ dumpster diver/

indie drummer. He would look so fly
on South Beach or a screensaver.

A Hunter's Point of the Liver

The TV tower on Twin Peaks
radiates malignant gumballs

into the forever fog. That shit
will give you Hodgkin's but let's pretend

it's safe and drive up there Valentine's Day
with three Pinot Noirs, and a rubber,
lover. We gotta go somewhere. Mt. Tam

with boxed fried chicken and Fat Tire; a flask
of Jack at Judah Street viewpoint? We know

there's a point to all these viewings.
Soon we'll have words to say, and *things*.
In Seacliff, tectonic shifts will pick off

the manses and flick them into
the Richmond District. Let's pretend they'll stay,

and reminisce, through red teeth, how we spilled
onto Baker Beach, climbed Land's End,
went Camera Obscuring. If we were

any farther from our families
we'd be in the sea. But we're still we.

You love Cabernet Sauvignon and you
should really consider medical school.

Brooks Brother

The psychic says in a past lifetime she was
his darling daughter. So much for the shtetl,
now he wears a seersucker suit: blue and blonde,
blonde and blueblooded.

A minyan of men spent their days davening
but he was at war with a mad god. Hashem
was his as much as he was anybody's
though the way it was

written made him feel like a farmer without
any rain. There was no hope in anything.
Only a question: Live or die? Live or die?
In or out a door?

On one side of the door there was a small bed
and beside the bed a basin where he washed up
her girl hands, washed and cried: *The skin, the muscle,
the yellow marrow.*

Next Year in Jerusalem

There are two men; one
is headed West for the boughs
of guacamole blossoms,
oodles of gurus, scotch

and prego starlets. If he were
any fairer he'd be vapor;
now you're crying dresses
in the snow, when the second says:

Hombre didn't take you
to dinner? That Pilgrim. I've got
potatoes from Bogotá
and a cross in my cock. You can

use it to bruise my bones
girlie, won't you let me be
your casket? He's crazy, and brown
as Jesus too. You've not seen

such charity, not in Pittsfield,
not in the Follies either
when they first sprung you from your box
like a police mouse, you can say

that again. Learn to drop
and relearn to drop. Embrace
the one who seeks you. The words
are *thank you*. Soon he'll pet

your cloche until the flower falls,
lick your little doll skull
to sunburn, a wolf in friendship,
fellowlike of lute. Guarding

your votive tomb, he'll have you
doing Ave Marias
to the sun, when you thought
there was something really wrong.

Not Quite Ready for the NRA

My first gun looks more glam on Shirlanne
and her cupcake-frosted, Daisy Duked, Prell girl
ambitions. I need Velveeta grits

and a thicker sexual history
to pull it off. Daddy's straight terrified
when I arrive at the trailer, blabberin'

about growin' myself some ranch charm, thing all shined
like lip gloss. Says it might go off. I plead:
Second Amendment! Down the highway

Hollywood is makin' a cult picture. A lady
best defend herself from those headcase actor boys.
What if some Lorenzo Lamas-lookin' motherfucker

trips the light fantastic and wants to do
a sex tape? He'll drag us to his compound, papered
woodgrain, make us drink LA sunshine. Could be

strychnine. All the pagan-types will be there
playin' dress-up with Casablancan feathers
and eatin' off Pu Pu platters. Their yoga moves

will intoxicate, the redheads pushin'
silicone served up on a cocaine spoon. His room
won't have no bible on the chaise lounger, only

a plate of raw oysters and Liz Taylor's
Oscar wig. What if he goes all out Clint Eastwood?
Sweet Jesus, let him draw blood.

The Bird

The guy I flipped off
in the chicken zip car was
Robert Zimmerman.

It was Gilligan,
Oedipus, it was your Aunt
Grace, Jack Kennedy,

a lop-eared bun bun
I forgot to feed for one
month. The roaches ate

its ashy dung drops
while it sighed, rotting alive,
back to embryo.

Everything rots
in downtown San Francisco
but I loved it so

with tics and itches.
I didn't mean to do it
with the whole corncob

f humanity.
 only wanted to ball
n someone else's

rive-in movie screen.
'm sorry Kennedy
leeding on Elm Street.

62

At His Aunt Sheila's in Taos

I lied. I spit out Aunt Sheila's peyote button
in the bathroom when I said I was just gonna spit
spit. I doubt you tripped either. You were shooting arrows

at flies that day as if to say: *not this, not this, nor this,*
playing it cool to the bitter taste of cactus pimples
like Frank Sinatra going down on an unwashed number.

I would need a trashcan full of those buggers to be sated.
Even at 19, I knew nothing would be enough
for my dis-ease. Not the cheese sandwiches in the backseat

or a bursting baggie of weed. Not the damiana
tincture or jars of organic peanut butter. Not enough
liquor or loose tobacco in all of New Mexico.

I was in pain in the place I peed, but scared to say.
You talked truth with Sheila on the back porch and Sheila said:
We're all one. That sent you snarking over your Hansen's cola.

Truth's relative, you said, *like money.* Of course, you had plenty.
But the truth was, if someone had told me: *Urinate*
after you have sex with him, hippie-rabbit, I wouldn't have

lain there on the clay floor, clutching my pelvis. The truth was
your Dad was a doctor who could call prescriptions
into Taos that would cool my canals and make me pee orange.

There was no way I would ask for it. Sheila massaged me
Hawaiian-style and diagnosed my energy blockages.
You store sadness in your feet, she said, *it's Sagittarius*

rising. Someday you'll learn to let things go. I did not ask:
But what about my urethra? Sheila was 46, thin,
invested in solar. She rolled tight spliffs and knew Grace Slick.

I let Sheila bathe me in rosewater, wrap me in hemp robes
and place me in front of the sunset like a TV.
Everybody said that I glowed like a firefly.

It's Just Registering

Again there are two men; one will buy me
western world *Araby*: psychotropic drugs,
sneakers and technology. He conspires

with my mother on a custom-made, platinum
taser, adorned with human bones torn
from the shins of hunters. Of course, my mother

is delighted. But I choose the other
and awake one morning spat out to a dark spot
on his couch. In the end there is going to be

no end. My doubts will bubble up as we drink
from mismatched cups and eat ten-minute pasta meals
forever. Even when the wedding brings complete

sets: butter dish, gravy boat, soup tureen,
champagne flutes, fusion juicing station, counter
barbecue, they will be the last of anything new.

Double Dubuque

She hit a new bottom when she couldn't opt
on a pair of flip flops. Hollywood rhinestone
or earth mother hemp? *This gal is no wellspring
of mental wellness,*

the saleslady said. She cried then. She drove
cross-country, with incense in the vents, alone
that summer. Such heavyweight states. Las Vegas
and Salt Lake City

rose out of darkness like neon snakes above
the interstate. A wild horse sanctuary
in Hot Springs and the red light ladies of Butte,
lacey and winking.

While she slept she dreamt the road and when she drove
she smoked menthols, Djarum cloves and good shit sold
behind a fireworks shop in Tennessee,
solid company,

her head a motel for the bohemian.
Like The Beats, she thought, smoothing the Travelodge
sheets, *in California they'll understand
mavericks like me.*

But Los Angeles was only more highway
on the flip side of the driver's side air bag.
In Marina del Ray the loneliness came,
an ancient handmaid.

Never Saw a Woman
after The Doors

She wants an island kitchen Christmas ham
and wealthy groom, or roadhouse bungalow
to hold the alley cigarette boy's hand
and rainy whiskey glasses for her bones.

The highway's full of dandies and motels,
a caravan of strangers in the sun.
The mansion's fat with pork and hostess belles
who watch L.A. on winter television.

Before the funeral comes she'll have two moods;
There are pills for quickness on the stormy road,
and when the clock parts vibrate in their wood
there are pills for sleep inside an actor's home.

Nut Hand
after Bob Dylan

I'm in the mood for a bust-up
at the farmer's market, Rachel Maddow
is so over me, and you too
Pacific Northwest, admit it.
Ring bell, hard to tell, oh guru

where are you now? Guru's in lotus pose
on the craps table at Caeser's Palace.
Guru sees the lights of Vegas
and forsakes the desert. Guru
got herself a brand new mullet.

What do you call a guru in the slammer?
A spiritual bottom. Why so funny?
Disdain for self. Guru, if I post
bail, do I remain teachable?
We can do uddiyana bandha

at the Westward Ho and I'll tell no one
about the sausage incident,
not even god. Once you did asana
in Paris. Here we have an Eiffel Tower
of our own. Here we levitate the ghost

of Liberace, stuffed on daiquiris.
Plug me back in. I see how little
time we get. Even the slots men,
whooping at sevens, are growing gray.
Let's ask questions of ourselves and they'll pay.

Who Loves Ya?

When the three poet ancestors, each named
Ann, fold me into their Bloomsbury Group
at a rooftop pool party, there's not
enough oxygen. They talk old guard—
jazz, ashtray, verb, Paris—and warn
against falling into fashion.

What if I don't take snifters? I ask.
Nowadays, Diet Coke's ok, says Ann.
I didn't try sweet vermouth, I say.
It's never too late in the day, says Ann.
Take a break from your scares, says Ann.
Or have them anthologized, says Ann.

The Anns' daughters emerge from behind
a plate of poached pears to tell me I'm blessed.
The Anns aren't jealous of my youth.
Look, they say, *none of them wear bathing suits.*
I think they must like me for my womb,
how it's pruned like theirs. But the Anns know

my first baby before I do.
Expensive and confusing, says Ann.
Symbiotic and fattening, says Ann.
It'll be no Ars Poetica, says Ann.

Amun and You

Amun the creator comes alone
into the night and makes the coasts.
Then he calls your cell phone, and says:

Honey, I spent all my money
on dirty martinis and speed,
building the globe. I've got nothing

left for tea. Get in my corner?
With a little love, we won't desire
plasma TVs or wireless routers.

And you say: *My Lord, kiss me*
on the lips. I never knew
you needed me like this.

Hey, Hey Paula

My favorite junkie
is out again tonight,
propped on the 6 train platform
scratching down her sores.

Turn the corner ramp
and her body surprises
like real vanilla ice cream
and dirty birthday presents.

What is the difference
between the Buddha
and the junkie?

She looks like a lama, lilting
in Lhasa, smiling
the half-smile of tranquil mind.

Buddhas and junkies want more
out of life than life
has to offer. Buddha
wants to want nothing.

Her chin is tattooed
with blue stars, and the role
of starving dog is played
tonight by starving dog.

She doesn't want pot roast
and mashed potatoes;
they will absorb the drug
or make her vomit out nirvana.

She's taking the sidewalk all the way
to methadone maintenance
and cotton fever.
Who wouldn't want to be her?

If you're obsessed you might call
yourself a junkie:
a Buddhism junkie,
a junkie junkie.

Buddha never injected
on Christmas Eve.
It's not enough
to smell her hair grease.

Everyday Essentials

Loaded reindeer hangs
rug pad and runner
both dishwasher and oven

safe, in a library
of caviar and cloves.
Eco-friendly latte

and flared trumpet, a glass
tulip, a granite cheese board,
what looks like snowflakes

in Swedish jewel tones
amuse bouche, then spiral gold
and silver bugle bells

breathing optic velvet.
Ruby red nut puts
the bubbly or martini

on antiqued mercury slate
and blends, sophisticated
baby, a threshold

to the holidays. Flocked trees
with mitered corners
and white-hot trim, dressed in tongue

and groove joinery,
with all the woodsy charm
of five fixed cupboard shelves,

poly-cotton blend, secure
the doors and tell us we're
good. Tell us we're good.

Dear Billy Collins

If I don't stop using
the word *fingerbang*
I'll never get to be

poet laureate.
Are mornings at your house
really that good? I should

start listening to more
Art Blakey. Is it in
your espresso or

does someone have to die
so I can get some
writing done? The jazz

isn't working
and sometimes I forget
to watch the world.

I should go over
to the Brooklyn Museum.
Once I used the word

touché incorrectly
for 24 years.
A stranger set me straight

and so I married him.
We need a wife
to cook us osso bucco.

Is it really that good?
Touché. The paintings
don't work and I don't think

I am enough. I should go
bald. Is it the rainfall
or must I have someone

else's shit childhood
so I can get some
writing done?

Pretend the Poet Ancestor Never Went to Rehab

Beat your own keppe
say: *lookee how prolific*
say: *she never quit a thing*
say: *she kept it at one*

evening in the 80s
in JR Ewing's Mercedes

(certainly a pearl necklace
was involved, oh yes, she surely
lost that Ferragamo footing
for the sake of Mars poetica)

yet somehow she landed
cerebrum-side up
the following morning
in the Ewing breakfast nook

(grapefruit of all things)

to say: *Miss Ellie,*
when the pupil is ready
say: *Miss Pamela, that's powerful*
use of enjambment
say: *now Sue Ellen, you're sweet*
on Ted Berrigan, admit it

and good hair was never so important.

When You Say One Thing but Mean Your Mother

He is the type
of lover who lolls
in Glimmerglass Park
at Beaver Pond
on Covered Bridge
breathing the ether.

This is his playtime
but not yours.
The great outdoors
unscheduled
makes you tremble.
You need to chew things.

The lover
was breastfed
by a sane woman
who cradled
her pregnant belly
for the camera.

Sane as animals.
The lover's mother
played her belly
Ella Fitzgerald
and it was;
it must have been
the wasness

that scared your mother
ballooning
past TV trays
ads for Grand Marnier
and radio waves

into who knows
how far out?
The doctors gave her
a Leo end date
but no yardstick.
You stayed longer

to Virgo
until she split
a maxi dress
at Bamberger's.
This was new
territory.

If they'd given her
a leather bit
and said: *Bite on this*
it's finite
you might have
been a rose.

Instead they shot her
with cosmic rays

and she twisted
from the mothership.
When she woke
they expected

she'd let you
suck her ducts
swaying and smacking
squeezing and latching
head cocked up.
Who were you?

Enfamil
and Similac
in tin cups
gave her shelter
from prickling fever
udder drain

scorpion sores
nipple trickles
and carpeted
the bedroom mirror
with cheek kisses
for Narcissus.

King James Approximately

Lately I'm practicing practicing god's will,
not my own, like the lusty astronaut

who drove a two-pound hammer drill from Houston
to Orlando, wearing a diaper

so she wouldn't have to pull over
before kidnapping her lover's wife.

I didn't think I'd live long enough
to see me still being me, but Saturn

returns with a teenage trick: steal packages
of fake meat from the deli counter and count

the slices aloud; then eliminate them
out the window of a speeding car, each piece

a gamey hood ornament: bologna
Jetta, ham Corolla, smoked turkey taxi.

How should I know god's will? I'm making choices
on crumpled pieces of fake meat tossed in the air.

In the old days, I knew it on my father's face
when he saw the bologna car, turned to me and stared.

They'll Never Stop Talking About Emily

What did she smell like?
>Dust and pheasant. The linens
>>must have really stunk

when she went catatonic.
>She would have made you sick

before you got her well.
>*She would fever for me*
>>*on yellow letters*

and call me Master. She'd flirt
by ignoring you—undo

the curtain tie-backs sudden.
>*But those hands-on burials,*
>>*the scones and shadows!*

Don't pretend life meant something
>then, and not now. Amherst

has Winter Fest. You can
>paddle Walden Pond
>>between Volvo wagons,

get busted in The Commons
        or have your brother's marriage.

You can be a lily pond
        for poems to land on;
                if you live in the city

be a parking spot.

Summer Soldiers

This is the game: we will gaze down the barrel
of our drugstore lipsticks, wait for you to finish

band practice. Stalk you in the 7-11 lot.
Where the boys are. Boys. Sparrow spirits on skateboards,

bottles of Tahitian Treat, Rose's Cola
and blue raspberry Slurpees laced with vodka.

We have the blues because we want to be you:
all shit-beers and stars, pentagrams instead of temple.

Old-school kick flips—no purses—under the low-hung moon,
and you can skin your knees and you can give us

carpet burn all evening in somebody's basement,
trying to lick our nothing-tits, baby lions

cleaning china plates. Calluses and nipples,
bass guitars. *Cinnamon gum will turn him on,*

say the wise women of *Seventeen* magazine.
What kind of kisser are you? Timid? Sexy? Strong?

Then you'll heelflip your Simples, ollie higher
over gutters, down suburb sidewalks, to your mothers

and we'll go tongue the mirror in your honor,
apply glitter eyeliner, make scars out of pimples.

Kundalini Blooper

Let's say you've seen monks in red robes roaming
the city all week: at Morimoto,

Asia De Cuba, Bergdorf Goodman—
a good omen? You swear you see your mother

but not her mouth. This woman could be
a danger to you and anybody

could be mother. There's lullabies
in strangers. It's stranger at home. The sofa

won't hold and you can't remember codes.
Within hours, Mother's thighs are yours.

Oyster Lover

She saw through her mascara,
as they walked rationally
in the snowplowed alley,
that there was nothing wrong
with taking a second lover.

In her doorway, the alchemy
of one bad oyster and six flights
of Johnny Walker straight
clogged his throat like black cake.
I'm going to be ill!—

and she was thrilled to watch
him spilling out his wilderness
on her floors. The letting go
was everywhere, from outer space
down to their underwear.

Romancing the Detox

You're nobody

till some sweet-faced junkie
with a Dixie cup of juice

and methadone loves you
more than his drugs

and this one, gorgeous, gagging boy
who died today in Tompkins Square,

again, ogles your war story
as he crawls his way to shit

and burp up bile
in the hospital bathroom.

What a charmer!
You could hug and dry hump

and he'd show you how to shoot up
movie myths under the Brooklyn Bridge.

Strays and sirens will spark the dark
as your slowing hearts

bid bye-bye to fraidy-cat
who never graduated

from capsules and canned heat
to say: *Chin chin! Bombs away!*

Let's really burst into flames!

Acknowledgments

Grateful acknowledgment is made to the journals in which some of these poems first appeared, sometimes in different forms:

Opium, Shampoo, The Del Sol Review, Conte, The Promethean, The Blue Jew Yorker, Flesh and *Because We Write*

Many thanks to my parents, Linda and Robert Broder (who promise not to read it), for your patience and support. To my publisher Jason Cook for making it happen, and to my editor Jesse Bradley for the skillful pruning. To Jason Schneiderman, David Groff, Elaine Equi, Leigh Hovey, Kara Cesare, Kate Garrick, Joseph Riippi and Ryan Davidson for your guidance and encouragement. To my sister, Hayley Broder, Shoshanna Must and Margaret Curry for your friendship. To Benjamin Gibson, Chauncey O'Neill and Brandon Finney for making it look foxy. To Jennifer L. Knox, Daniel Nester and Matthew Rohrer for believing in the cause. And once again to Nicholas Poluhoff, for love and editing.

Printed in the USA
CPSIA information can be obtained
at www.ICGtesting.com
LVHW041543210424
778013LV00028B/677